Pass *the* Pulpit

Pass *the* Pulpit

The Ultimate Test of Ministry

D. K. Samu-el, Sr.

XULON PRESS

Xulon Press
2301 Lucien Way #415
Maitland, FL 32751
407.339.4217
www.xulonpress.com

© 2022 by D. K. Samu-el, Sr.

All rights reserved solely by the author. The author guarantees all contents are original and do not infringe upon the legal rights of any other person or work. No part of this book may be reproduced in any form without the permission of the author.

Due to the changing nature of the Internet, if there are any web addresses, links, or URLs included in this manuscript, these may have been altered and may no longer be accessible. The views and opinions shared in this book belong solely to the author and do not necessarily reflect those of the publisher. The publisher therefore disclaims responsibility for the views or opinions expressed within the work.

Unless otherwise indicated, Scripture quotations taken from the King James Version (KJV)–*public domain.*

Paperback ISBN-13: 978-1-6628-8814-4
Ebook ISBN-13: 978-1-6628-8815-1

Foreword

In act 1, scene 1 of Shakespeare's *Hamlet*, Francisco the night watchman cries out to the oncoming figure in the dark, "Stand and unfold yourself." In our modern translation, Francisco is requesting that the person reveal himself to him. Much like the night watchman in the his *Twelfth Night*, I have been tasked with the privilege of helping unfold and reveal to you the character of our author, Superintendent Demetrius K. Samu-el, Senior Pastor of the Historic Sherman Memorial Church of God in Christ in Charlotte, North Carolina.

Pastor Samu-el has always been a gifted orator. As a teenager in the city of Buffalo, New York, his talents were showcased during the city's Annual Martin Luther King, Jr. Citywide Celebration. The crowd that was assembled in the famed Kleinhans Music Hall was enraptured by Samu-el's powerful rendition of the classic "I Have a Dream" speech. This gifted young man was also a finalist in his school district's senior-high-school speaking contest. It was evident that Samu-el would make a powerful impact in the world as he matured and developed.

Sometime in the early 1990s, I got to know Samu-el through an arranged encounter orchestrated by another pastor while attending a conference of the Church of God in Christ (COGIC). The pastor introduced us to each other because he felt that as young men coming up in the church, we should know each other and perhaps develop a friendship. What neither of us knew then was how that arranged meeting would turn into an incredible friendship and brotherhood of over thirty years and counting. It has been my great honor to watch Samu-el grow into the powerful leader and teacher of the Bible that he is today.

We started out as young ministers together navigating the pathways and politics of the Grand Ole Church of God in Christ. We each became ordained elders and then married our respective soulmates within months of each other. I am honored to be listed among those Pastor Samu-el—or as we affectionately refer to him in private moments, "Meet"—calls a friend. Truly, Meet is a man after God's own heart. He is a humble servant of the Lord and a compassionate giver of his time, talents, and treasure.

As you read through the pages of this book, you will come to appreciate the incisive and thought-provoking style that Samu-el employs to educate and illuminate our understanding of God's divine purpose in our lives. In fact, I am reminded of a time when I sat in the audience during one of Pastor Samu-el's speaking engagements in which he broke down the etymology of the word *educate*. He shared that it came from the Latin term *educere*, which means "to lead, draw out." With the turning of each page and delving into each chapter, you will experience how this author draws out revelations and insights that may have been previously hidden from your conscious mind.

As Pastor Samu-el unfolds his personal journey with you, you will catch glimpses of our collective humanity shining through some of these experiences. You will be able to relate and have those head-nodding moments of confirmation. This book will also challenge you to be introspective and examine yourself in the light of God's purpose and vision for your life. You will have to give an account of the things that you are doing now, and you must consider how or whether they are preparing you for your next.

This book is by no means a fairy tale filled with happy talk and dreams that come to fruition based on hopes and wishes. To be clear, this book is bound together by a lifetime of peaks and valleys whose crossings have demonstrated the awesomeness of God in the life of a yielded vessel. Pastor Samu-el shares both the practical and the spiritual elements necessary to live out a life of purpose. God requires holiness and humility. Pastor Samu-el's experiences have provided him with good doses of both

Foreword

to help him communicate how we can cultivate these essential pillars in our lives and in our churches.

When Pastor Samu-el asked me to write the foreword for this book, I was profoundly moved to be able to contribute to this incredible endeavor. I have always shared with him that he is indeed a giant among men. It is not simply his physical stature, but his vast intellect that warrants this analogy. To see this work come together and to be a part of this tremendous effort brings me a deep sense of joy as Pastor Samu-el shares this powerful message with you. Don't just buy this book, but pick up one for your friend or loved one as well, so that you all can talk about what you're learning together and how you will apply the lessons to live out your purpose.

If you are sincerely looking to answer the question *Why am I here?* then you've got a good start in your hands to help you search out your path to true fulfillment. As Pastor Samu-el has often asked,

How is 'going there,' going to tell 'been there,' how to get there?

Allow Pastor Samu-el, who has been there, to help you on your journey to getting there.

Elder Kenya K. Hobbs, MAOL
President,
Empowering Everyday Women's Ministries, Inc.

Dedication

This book is dedicated to all those who pushed me to it, especially in those days when I couldn't see it being a reality; to every person who can find in my story the solace and strength to persevere through theirs:

Here's to passing the test!

Acknowledgments

Thank you to my wife and children, who have been my number one fans: Catherine, Demetrius ("Junior"), and Denae ("Princess Kailah").

Mother, I *finally* did it. You've reminded me every day that this is the other part of my life's purpose.

To the greatest church in the whole wide world, the Historic Sherman Memorial Church Of God In Christ (HSMCOGIC), and to the Fantastic Four, we'll ever be the Fabulous Five with me.

To my beta readers, your observations and critiques helped tremendously.

Thank you to Missionary Crystal Poston, the eagle-eyed editor extraordinaire.

And to the one and only Elder Kenya K. "Dr." Hobbs, sir, your contributions were priceless and, I pray, immortal.

Introduction

It has been said that the bar exam is the most difficult test to take. Depending upon who is asked, the Graduate Record Examination (GRE) or the Securities Exchange Commission (SEC Series 7 exam) would come second to any of the states' bar exams. I have taken neither the GRE nor a bar exam, but I have taken the Series 7 exam to obtain a brokerage license. What makes the Series 7 exam so hard is the fact that one is expected to know the "most correct" answer to questions that have been designed so each one has more than one right answer to it. Many questions that arise in our lives have straightforward answers; others are not so black and white. For the shades-of-gray scenarios, dependency on more than intellect is absolutely essential. Life has a way of yielding an awesome return on the investment of experience. Experience is still the best teacher. One of the most prolific pearls of wisdom I gained from my counselor several years ago is this: preach the Word of God—avoid situational and political rhetoric. As a young person, I exercised the wisdom instilled in me to not try to tell parents how to raise teenage children—or couples what fifty years of marriage is like—but there are some instances when divine inspiration takes precedence.

The pulpit is a test of knowledge, emotional and psychological stability, spiritual conviction and persuasive prowess, doctrinal proofs, integrity, faith, and most of all, character. The call to service is more than a notion. In fact, Jesus said that many are called, but few are chosen. It is the chosen one who passes the test of the pulpit. The called can lead God's people only so far. The called, we have seen, fall and fail, even the mightiest of them. Why? Because they have not made their calling *and* their election sure. This test is more than an entry examination; it knows no end except death. It is the process of election that separates the men from the boys, so to speak. This is where the heat of drive and the depth of compassion are proven. This is where the proof of love and devotion to God has to be stronger than the will to please people. It must be stronger than the desire to succumb to the temptation of self-aggrandizement.

You cannot lead people where you have not gone or are not willing to go.

For as long as the children of Israel wandered in the wilderness, at least one of them was not lost. Moses had spent the previous forty years learning the very territories that the Israelites covered the forty years following.

For several years prior to becoming a pastor, I was the ministerial staff leader at the church where I served. My initiation was rough, to say the least. First, I was the youngest ordained elder on the board at the time of my appointment. To be made the leader over a group of men, some of whom had been preaching longer than I had even been alive, was . . . well, let's just say intimidating. Nevertheless, I had an assignment, one that I'd accepted and was not willing to be defeated at.

There were countless lessons I learned during my tenure there. On one hand, many lessons were simply teaching me what *not* to do and how *not* to mishandle God's people. On the other hand, much knowledge was transferred from an experienced leader who understood the fragility of the human psyche and emotions. There was quite a bit to know about the hierarchy of the church. Just as in any viable organization, structure is a required element if there is to be any level of success expected. Everybody is subject to somebody, and we all must be subject to the lordship of Christ.

The pulpit is where the gospel is preached, where the good news pronounced. The pulpit is *not* a place for the faint of heart or for the uncompassionate. Once you have crossed into it, you have passed *the point of no return*.

INTRODUCTION

It may be hard, but it is not impossible to do. Pass the pulpit while passing the pews is getting by on margin and skipping over merit. Too many are passing the pews to get to the pulpit. Whom will they minister to? Preaching and teaching is only a fraction of the minister's responsibility. You cannot effectively minister to anyone until you have sat with their pain. Passing the pulpit successfully *is* the Great Commission!

Assignment-driven leaders are not sidetracked by the glitz and glamour of ministry. Neither are they turned off by the guts and gore of grassroots servitude. There is a high cost to be paid in order to be effective and remain relevant in working for the upbuilding of the kingdom of God. I am afraid that the generations after mine will have too low of an expectation of true ministry. The diminishing presence and reverence for the elders is an area of major concern. Unless they are taught, how will they ever know?

This book is designed as a navigational tool and encouragement to press past what you see in order to tap into what you know. Let's experience the fulfillment of what it means to *Pass the Pulpit: The Ultimate Test of Ministry*!

Contents

Foreword vii
Dedication xi
Acknowledgments xiii
Introduction xv

Chapters

1. The Measure of a Man 1
2. Resisting the Temptation to Quit 9
3. Brother's Keeper—Blessed Be the Tie That Binds 15
4. Precious Stones 19
5. Testing Time 25
6. Called. Equipped. Sent. 35
7. The Cost of Greatness 41
8. Dangers of Premature Exposure 47
9. Silence Is Consent . . . But to What? 55

About the Author 59

One

The Measure of a Man

A GOOD name is better than precious ointment: and the day of death than the day of one's birth. Better is the end of a thing than the beginning thereof: and the patient in spirit is better than the proud in spirit. (Ecclesiastes 7:1, 8 emphasis added)

For many the question is, *How do I measure up?* It is a question that, unfortunately for some, may never really be satisfied. In fact, it can ultimately end up being a question that adversely affects several areas of life. If it is allowed to, it can become gnawingly consuming. The pursuit of uncovering its truth must not drive an individual into unnecessary duress. As challenging as it can be, it may not be as pertinent or even as threatening as it may seem. Light shone in any dark place exposes its composition and elements. Knowledge truly is power. Power in the right hands is handled with care. From those hands, it is dispersed wisely and distributed to the needy, those who would most benefit from its wealth. In awakening, many mysteries have been made plain. The successful end of seeking answers means the process is resolved with enlightenment through discovering that it really is not as vital to know as we may have thought. If during the process we gain the necessary assurance of defining ourselves by and for ourselves (with God's help, of course), then we have done well. It is then that the separation of the confident from the contentious is clearly defined.

Measuring up can be a truly daunting task. By whose standards does one measure? What is it that one measures against, by what gauge or proverbial measuring stick? The Word of God seems to suggest that if there be anything to measure against or define one's worth by, it *must* be by how much one has done with what they were graced to do. So now the question becomes, *What is my purpose of being?* This is probably by far one of the most frequently asked questions ministers (pastors in particular) are faced with. Of course, if anybody can answer it, certainly it ought to be a spiritual leader, right? Ironically, that leader may very well be asking themselves that same question. The individual the question is addressed to is expected to also be the defining point or at least to be able to give solid direction.

Introspection may not be the best solution. Why not? We are ever-evolving creatures. There are discoveries we make about ourselves at every age and stage of our lives. Though soul-searching may be beneficial, it may not be exact. To know precisely what God has assigned and purposed in Himself for you, it is necessary to consult the source, your creator. Perhaps one of the greatest examples of one who had success in doing so is the apostle Paul, who settled once he had the revelation that to die is to gain by continuing to live is Christ.

If the search is derived through reflection, the desired result should be that God sees Himself when He looks back. What others should see when they look at a believer is the express image of God. How so? Actions more often speak louder than words. Seeing yourself as God sees you can only happen because you know how He sees you. That, my friend, is accomplished because of right relationship. Seeing God by the deeds done in the body—the extension of kindness, attributes of love, and the evident maturity of selflessness—displays Him vividly to those who doubt His existence and makes Him more real to those who know Him.

Either way, whether through introspection or reflection, *How do I measure up?* becomes more relevant when held under the microscope. The truth of the matter is this: the whole duty of humanity is to fear God and to keep His commandments.

Fearing God goes further than reverencing Him in his God-ness. It is bigger than being afraid of Him. To fear God means to live a life pleasing unto Him, a life of worship, a life of witness, a life of devotion. A life devoted to God is not unleashed authorized weirdness. The one thing that concerns me most about this generation is the grave lack of respect and fear of the Almighty. Society has done a masterful job of making God a "nice guy." In the meantime, He has been humanized in the eyes of too many. It has ushered in the philosophy that when God does what we want Him to, He is good. When bad things happen, He does not exist. And for what we do not understand, He then is reduced to being considered a trickster. Even mainstream Christianity has bought into the idea of a god of convenience. This leaves it to those who are in relationship with Him to present and represent Him to the world.

We cannot keep His commandments if we know not what they are.

It is extremely important that as a minister of the gospel, you have secured a genuine relationship with the God you testify of. Having a personal relationship with Christ is necessary. As elementary as that may sound, so many have made their way to the pulpit without going in the most direct route. This is a disservice to the body of Christ and damaging to the efforts to promote the kingdom of God. It has caused mass confusion and in some cases hysteria and even the loss of human life.

How then shall they call on him in whom they have not believed? And how shall they believe in him of whom they have not heard? And how shall they hear without a preacher? And how shall they preach, except they be sent? As it is written, How beautiful are the feet of them that preach the gospel of peace, and bring glad tidings of good things!
(Romans 10:14–15)

Wolves in sheep clothing is a very real thing. Pulpit pimps and thirst traps are real. They are real, but are they avoidable? Are they conquerable?

Yes, why yes, they are! It begins with an intolerance for foolishness from those in authority, followed up with a strong commitment from fellow laborers in the work of the Lord. A system of accountability is nothing new, just unheard of in some arenas. It is just as necessary for us today as it was for the Twelve who walked with Jesus then.

For over a decade now, I have subscribed to my own theory of assets and liabilities, using this verse from Proverbs, *"Iron sharpeneth iron; so a man sharpeneth the countenance of his friend"* (Prov. 27:17) as my gauge of choice. I typically consider myself to be a pretty good judge of character. Having thus said, and I do not believe it should take a long time to figure out whether the connections I make in life will be for the good or a waste of time, energy, and/or effort. Of course, there are almost always exceptions to the rules. So far, my judgment has proven to be quite successful. God has favored me with some of the most phenomenal friends anyone could ask for. Though I have decided not to live by the dictates of another, I can honestly say that I have found what others think of me to be expedient in how I continue improving on my "me-ness."

Though we encounter people daily, not all of them are connections, and even more so, most are not for commitments, at least not lifelong ones. Our obligation in securing friendships is easy: *he that will have friends must show himself friendly*. It does not just happen to any of us. God, behind the scenes, does these divine setups. I believe all our personal destinies are connected to someone else's. As human beings, we are inextricably bound to one another.

Before I say what the measure of a man is, let me first say what it is not. It is not what people call you—it's what you answer to. Even with having the scriptural knowledge of God (*"For God has not given us the spirit of fear"*), we somehow still have the capacity from time to time to allow ourselves to be gripped by the strongholds of fear. In real time, the enemy of our soul can help us to look at our inadequacies and insecurities as every reason why we can't or shouldn't. I have discovered many times that the factor of intimidation has a way of camouflaging itself as humility. In essence it is false humility, which translates into pride. How prideful is it to believe that God, in choosing you, made a mistake? After all, pride means to be conscious of one's own dignity or worth. Funny thing, deciding your own worth contradictory to the valuation placed on your existence by the one who created you is quite bold, to say the least.

Not knowing the *why* does not prohibit one's ability to agree with or see the *what*. Grappling with understanding your purpose and coming to terms with the greatness you are called to are two very distinctly different things. In the immortal words of Nelson Mandela,

"Our deepest fear is not that we are inadequate. Our deepest fear is that we are powerful beyond measure." Meredith, M. (1997). *Nelson Mandela: A Biography*.

How do I measure up? Who's in charge of the calculation? Who sets the standard? More importantly, the question is, Why does it really matter? Everything is not a competition. Life is complicated enough. It has enough twists and turns to occupy more real estate in our minds than the space available.

In my opinion, one of the greatest tactics the enemy can ever use is distraction. Distraction is the thing that keeps us from focus. The devil knows that if you ever become focused, you will gain clear insight on where you are and where you're going. Once that happens, you'll immediately start setting boundaries and ultimately goals. Goals achieved, in turn, become milestones. Milestones are marks left behind as indicators of progress, indicators of success, indicators of missions completed.

Established boundaries restrict movement or advancement of nonessentials and reinforces prioritization of the essentials. Doing what is necessary is doing the most important things in order of priority. Making yourself a priority is not a sin. Now, that is a truth I have not known for very long. Yet it is a truth as liberating today as it was when I first heard it. Years and years of putting others' needs ahead of mine prohibited me from knowing what to do when there was no one to take care of but Me. What a journey! First, since I did not know Me, I did not know what

I liked, nor did I even know if I liked Me. Again, I did not know Me. Second, I was not sure if I was ready for the introduction. As it turns out, I was who I have always been the whole time. It was learning how to be Me unapologetically and currently becoming distinctively Me that fueled the continued evolution.

Will the real you dare to stand up?

While living behind the shadows of great men, the metamorphosis of Me began, or as my son calls it, the "evolution of Samu-el." It has been so much easier to define myself by what I have done. As you can imagine, different stages of life have been plagued by different versions of Me. Just as different as things seem to have been, they are much the same as they ever were. The one constant in my life is the fact that I have, am, and have always been a caregiver. As needs arise, so also has my level of response. Rising to the occasion has been rewarding. It also comes with its challenges, namely, the challenge of rediscovery.

The life lessons I have learned these last thirty-plus years are priceless. Being slung into the proverbial lions' den a few times and surviving has a way of developing character like nothing else. In the words of that good gospel song that I heard growing up, "I wouldn't take nothing for my journey now."

What you know will make you go. What you hear will make you fear. What you see will make you flee.

It's not revelation until it's revelation to you. We are all motivated by something. Knowing what moves you helps to expose what stagnates your progress as well. Knowledge is power, so get all the power you can. It is what you know that will propel you into your destiny. Knowing that God is sovereign, always aware of where you are and for you, will make you unstoppable. Having that kind of power gives you the advantage over present circumstances. Hearing with the right attitude and right spirit will make you fear with the right kind of fear. Reverential fear pulverizes fear of the unknown like an elephant walking on peanut hulls. Seeing through the eyes of faith grants you the urgency of being present in the moment—right here, right now. It is no wonder God does not allow us to see the whole picture at once. The ministry of presence allows us to serve currently and to serve relevantly.

It has been my discovery that layers of faith are only uncovered as necessary. It is not until a certain kind of faith is needed that it is summoned to the forefront. It amazes me how many times I've thought I had met my limit, only to realize that I had a greater capacity to continue. Pressure is your friend! As unwelcome as it may be, pressure is the only way to truly discover what is in you. Life's vices will squeeze out of you all that is needed to thrive, if you allow its due process.

Stay with me as we walk through this essay together. Along the way I will share my personal testimony and a few nuggets of wisdom that have helped me to remain focused on the main thing.

Jesus says to Peter, *"And the Lord said, Simon, Simon, behold, Satan hath desired to have you, that he may sift you as wheat: But I have prayed for thee, that thy faith fail not: and when thou art converted, strengthen thy brethren"* (Luke 22:31–32). God in His infinite wisdom has synchronized our lives so intricately that there are certain people we encounter in lives who have been strategically placed for the purpose of helping us to our next. When you are converted . . . when you realize who you are . . . when you come to grips with your purpose . . ., strengthen your brother. In other words, make sure you help someone else discover their purpose. We all have one. Some learn what theirs is sooner in life. Others of us need a little extra help getting to it.

Just as each of us has purpose, we each have a voice also. Your voice must be heard. Be sure, however, when you use your voice, it is for good. *"Death and life are in the power of the tongue: and they that love it shall eat the fruit thereof"* (Prov. 18:21). It really does matter what we say. Our words have power—power to heal or to kill. We must also keep in mind how important it is to exercise wisdom when we speak. We can say the right thing at the wrong time. Just because it is the truth does not mean it is not harmful. Many times when speaking the truth, it should be seasoned with grace. Of course, that's assuming you are interested in that truth landing right.

Sanitize your accent.

Accent is "a distinctive mode of pronunciation of a language, especially one associated with a particular nation, locality, or social class" (dictionary.com). Your accent is a telltale sign of where you have either come from or have been for a considerable amount of time. Newscasters and other individuals in broadcast media use certain techniques to disguise their voices so that people won't know where they are from. As it relates to ministry, your accent or the lack thereof will greatly determine the effectiveness of your witness. How will they know you? By how you show up!

Presentation is everything. How you show up must be intentional and purposeful. Showing up at the right time needs to be married to showing up at the right place and doing the right thing. They are waiting for *you*.

Two

Resisting the Temptation to Quit

> And it came to pass after a while, that the brook dried up, because there had been no rain in the land.
> (1 Kings 17:7)

What do you do when the brook has dried up? Prepare to move! God never intended for Elijah to become totally dependent upon His provision. My friend, we must never allow the things that God has blessed us with to take priority over our relationship with Him. Be vigilant. Remain focused on the provider, no matter how wonderful the provision is. When Elijah's comfort level sank to complacency, God did for him what He did for the children of Israel when it was time to move from Kadesh-Barnea. He sounded the alarm. He sent His word.

Rather than giving up, the goal should be to discover the why from the what. I heard a sermon many years ago titled "Why Not Me?" It is very human to revert to the "why me?" litany in hard times. I get it. I have been there. I have done that. In retrospect, I have wondered what if. What if I had not given up there? Thank God He already knows what we are going to do before we act. Furthermore, He does not allow our mistakes to define us, nor does He allow them to cancel us out. However, resisting the temptation to quit must come from within. That means there must be a root of hope.

Hope builds future expectations from past experiences. Where you have been has very much to do with where you are going. I am a firm believer that whatever we experience in life is a direct result of what we are purposed to do on this planet. And you already have within your all the necessary ingredients to make you whoever the Creator has planned for you to become in order for you to bring about His desired plan your life work together.

In 1 Kings 17, Elijah found himself in isolation after a great public demonstration of God's miraculous power. As bold as he was in calling on the God who answers by fire, you would think that he would continue in that vein and gloat for a while in how mightily God showed up for him; not so, instead, he found himself hiding. Apparently, it was not his idea, but also not against his will. The voice that guided him to the showdown at Mount Carmel is the same voice that told him to go hide himself by the brook Cherith.

The wonderful thing about our God is how He provides for His own. Elijah went to the brook without reservation. Why? He was given a promise with these directions: "And it shall be, that thou shalt drink of the brook; as I have commanded the ravens to feed thee there. So he went and did according unto the word of the Lord" (1 Kings 17:4–5). Wait! Not only did He tell him what he was getting into, but He let Elijah know that He would use a carnivorous bird, a "dirty bird," to feed him. God will use the most unlikely candidates to feed you what He would keep from you under other circumstances!

If we are honest, many times quitting feels like the best option, and often it feels like the only option, even when we know it really is not an option at all. The psalmist penned these words: *"From the end of the earth will I cry unto thee, when my heart is overwhelmed: lead me to the rock that is higher than I"* (Ps. 61:2).

Sometimes life hits so fast and hard that we do not have time to adjust our posture, to twist and turn to ready ourselves to receive the blows. One thing I have come to appreciate through it all is the worth of faith. When faith is given room to do what it is supposed to do, the process is activated. Process is how we attain mobility in the kingdom. If ever we are to move (in a progressive way), it is a process.

Resisting the Temptation to Quit

*And let us not be weary in well doing:
for in due season we shall reap, if we faint not.*
(Galatians 6:9)

Fainting immediately disqualifies you from the reaping process. Stay alert; your soul won't have to look back and wonder how you made it over. It is God's desire that you see His handiwork. He wants you to know just how real your deliverance is. As an eyewitness, you can tell others of the credibility and power of our God.

The evolution of Samu-el

Let the evolution begin! My son is very quiet. He is the kind of quiet that those who know just know that he is thinking about something. In one of his routine checkups on me to see where I was in the process of finishing this book, he sat back in his chair and said, "Ah, the evolution of Samu-el." We had a good laugh, but in a more somber moment, I had to admit it was a very good observation. The more I began to write, the more memories surfaced. It was in that moment that I asked his permission to share his story. There are a lot of things we have not talked about. It is not because he would not, but because I was not ready. Before I tell you his story, allow me to tell you a little more of mine. They connect like a huge jigsaw puzzle.

In 1994 I preached my initial sermon. It was titled "You've Come Too Far from Egypt to Turn Back Now" (Ex. 14:1–14). Who knew that today was coming other than God? There I was, a twenty-year-old kid who thought he knew a thing or two about life. Thank God I did what I was taught. That was, in the words of my pastor, "Stick with the script, son." He taught me from the very beginning of my ministry not to try to teach life lessons beyond my experience (unless, like the apostle Paul, there was divine inspiration) and to steer clear of what I was unsure of or not knowledgeable of. The pastor would often remind me of the seven sons of Sceva in Acts which says: "And the evil spirit answered and said, Jesus I know, and Paul I know; but who are ye? And the man in whom the evil spirit was leaped on them, and overcame them, and prevailed against them, so that they fled out of that house naked and wounded" (Acts 19:15–16). That's a scary thought; nevertheless, one to be considered.

In that initial sermon, I remember walking through the excitement the children of Israel expressed at the announcement of being freed from slavery. It was not long before their excitement became contaminated with fear and doubt. Here it was that God (answering their prayer) was releasing them from what was familiar, however uncomfortable, to an unknown, unfamiliar place—uncharted territory. As it turns out, they were more afraid of trusting God for something new than they were desperate for change. After escaping Egypt, the children of Israel were immediately faced with the mighty Red Sea. They approached their first obstacle at the border. What appeared to be the thing that would prohibit them from advancing is the very thing God chose as a testament of their faith. He proved to them that they already had what they needed in order to win. Remember, if He called you to it, He has equipped you to survive it.

It is our appetite for more, or for better, that causes us to pursue it. All it really takes is the desire to continue reaching for more in order to increase the chances of it happening. Resisting the temptation to quit is something we all will face in various stages of life. It is very much part of the human experience. Let's take another look at Elijah at the brook. I like to refer to his experience at the brook Cherith as "Swamp University." It was there that he learned what he needed to know about God for the next phase of his life and ministry.

My takeaway is this: not only will God use unexpected methods and means to provide for you, He will use you in unexpected ways to accomplish His mission. Elijah's willingness to submit to the process expedited his progress. For the children of Israel, they had to make the conscious choice to either retreat and go back into bondage or focus on the promised land and go on to freedom.

"And Moses said unto the people, Fear ye not, stand still, and see the salvation of the LORD, which he will shew to you to day: for the Egyptians whom ye have seen to day, ye shall see them again no more for ever. The LORD shall fight for you, and ye shall hold your peace" (Ex. 14:13–14). Because His thoughts are not ours, standing still is our best move. As simple as these instructions were, apparently there were some in the congregation who found it a bit challenging. Letting go of the logical or practical can be a daunting task for thinkers, but it is what faith requires in order to be activated. That's where He is calling us to—a place of faith. Beloved, that's where you want to go. Go there!

How ironic that the vehicle God chose to transport His people across the Red Sea was for them to stand still. That gives us to know that His "stand still" does not look like ours. His stand still is not static or stationary; it is depending on Him for every move.

Final observation . . . Notice that the Father told the children of Israel exactly what would happen if they were obedient: "If you . . . then I."

Stand still and see! Watch God do what He promised.

Three

Brother's Keeper—Blessed Be the Tie That Binds

I am distressed for thee, my brother Jonathan: very pleasant hast thou been unto me: thy love to me was wonderful, passing the love of women.
(2 Samuel 1:26)

The simplicity of this passage is David's candor. The complexity of it is that not many, especially men, will allow themselves to wholeheartedly trust another. Though a few things go without saying, others are better stated; otherwise, they go misunderstood. Baring our innermost feelings and thoughts leaves even the greatest among us most vulnerable. Vulnerability or total exposure is by far one of the most uncomfortably compromising positions one could ever find oneself in. When others see us as we really are, what will they think? There are far too many lines of distinction in the body of Christ. Most boundaries are denominational barriers and doctrinal discrepancies that we have allowed to creep into the body of Christ that have caused irreparable damage in many cases.

The story of David and Jonathan is by far one of the greatest examples of true friendship recorded in history. The strength of their bond was their vulnerability. We all need someone we can be completely transparent with.

The Bible tells another story in the book of Genesis about two brothers by the names of Cain and Abel. Cain was a groundskeeper and Abel a herdsman. They were the first sons born to Adam and Eve. The time came when God required of them an offering. He was not asking for just an offering, but for a sacrifice, which is an offering or gift of expense. God was expecting from them their best. After all, it was His best that they had to select from. When the time came for the presentation of gifts, the real character of the brothers was exposed. Abel brought before the Lord a conscious and thoughtfully considerate gift. Cain brought one that was not very desirable. In turn, God loved Abel's gift and had no respect for what Cain had brought to Him. When Cain got the bad news, he immediately felt hatred for his brother. Instead of doing a self-check, Cain felt threatened by one whom he now considered to be the competition. The next thing that happened was the world was introduced to its first murderer. Cain took revenge against God by killing his own brother. When God called him into question: "Where is your brother, Abel?" Cain responded with a question of his own: "Am I my brother's keeper?"

"Am I my brother's keeper?" has become the *absolutely relative* question of the ages. We are of all men most deprived if we alienate ourselves from the fellowship that God intended for us to participate in. How shall we ever truly know ourselves unless we first come to the realization that each of us needs help to overcome our common affliction? If by chance the heart decided that the rest of the body was unworthy of the blood it pumped, surely we would be in a most critical position. Every member in the body has a responsibility and part in the proper functioning of the body. No one job performed by any particular member is of any greater importance than the task carried out by another because it takes the collaborative efforts of these members to sustain this precious gift of life.

We must first understand it is imperative that we as a people become more concerned about the plight of our extended family. We must strive to see the good in each individual, and then we must learn how to channel that good to be mutually beneficial to the entire family. Life is pleasant and fulfilling when we collectively work at making it so. Going to the deep places within ourselves taps into the streams of compassion within us. In order to reach those depths, much digging is required. To reach the depths of others, we first have to visit the depths of ourselves. That requires self-discovery and the abandonment of superficial living. Many times it is so much easier to sit in a seat of judgment than to come down, deal, and show our scars. Admittedly, we pulpiteers rarely have the occasion to be brutally honest—even with each other.

Relatively speaking, my brother is an extension of myself, and I am inextricably bound to him by reason of a blood relationship. Yet, we have the opportunity to be redefined by blood by the miracle of the birth, death, burial, and resurrection of Jesus Christ. Therefore, we are at once bound and set apart by the blood relationship.

The ties that bind us are greater than the words that separate us. The letter killeth!

The deeds that men do in the dark are quite different from the creative works that God does in places no one can see. Motives are important. They matter greatly because motives fuel our actions. I am reminded of an anecdote. There was a young man laughing uncontrollably at an old man who was struggling to walk. The old man said to him, "Son, I really wish you could walk a mile in my shoes." The young man laughingly replied, "I can't even fit in your shoes!" The old man raised his eyebrows, nodded his head subtly, and said, "That's what I know. That's what I know."

On Memorial Day, May 25, 1992, my maternal grandmother passed away. We were very close. That was an extremely difficult time in my life. She had been there from day one. Her passing left a huge void. As I was attempting to pick up the pieces and move forward, I was introduced to four friends who have been with me ever since. At the end of a statewide summer youth convention I had been attending, the conference leader approached me and asked me to hang around for a few minutes because he wanted to do something. I did as he asked. A few minutes later he came back with three other young men. He asked the four of us to wait a moment because he was looking for one more to bring into the circle. We stood there making small talk while we waited for him to return. When he came back with the fifth brother, the conference leader began explaining why he thought it was a great idea for us to connect and exchange contact information. He took advantage of the opportunity to share with us that this was how the current leaders of the conference began their relationship many years prior. A senior leader saw them and introduced them to each other. Those five young ministers all ended up married, pastoring, and were still friends deep into adulthood. That day our little crew became the "Fabulous Five."

I often refer to these brothers like the four who carried their friend to Jesus on his sickbed. They have helped me through some very dark seasons in life. In turn, I have had the privilege of returning the favor. There have been times that they have ripped off roofs and lowered me down past the crowd to get to Jesus. And the times when I would have given up, they refused to let me.

More than thirty years later, we are all ministers of the gospel, accountability partners, and most of all, friends. Having a solid support system means so much in this line of work.

Four

Precious Stones

*And they shall be mine, saith the L*ORD *of hosts, in that day
when I make up my jewels; and I will spare them,
as a man spareth his own son that serveth him.*
(Malachi 3:17)

After the first failed pregnancy, we were reluctant and not at all enthusiastic about trying again. Somehow, through the justifiably deep apprehension, faith in God spoke louder than the noise of doubt. After about a year, we received the news of a successful conception. However, we were advised that it would not be wise to share the good news publicly until at least getting past the first trimester. Not a problem! Into the second trimester and after our enthusiastic announcement to everyone we knew to tell came the news that it was very likely that my wife would be incapable of carrying to full term. Ouch.

We immediately reverted to what we knew to do. That was to intensify our prayer time. I refused to believe that God would allow us to get this far along to be devastated again. This time my prayer was, "Lord, show me what my part in this is. I promise to follow Your instructions to the letter." He said plainly to me, "Trust me." My self-righteousness rose quickly with a question: "When have I not trusted You?" Uh-oh, it was only a matter of time until the Holy Spirit took me on a journey down memory lane. At this point, I had been telling others for years to trust God and have faith in God (with great conviction and a strong, stern voice at that. But without realizing it, at the same time I had more confidence in my own abilities and my family than I did in God. Talk about a tough pill to swallow.

Much like Job, there had been a hedge around me. I cannot remember a time in my life, prior to getting married and moving from Buffalo, New York, to Charlotte, North Carolina, that there was not someone waiting on guard and ready to jump in to help if it faintly looked as if I was about to holler for help.

Here we were, almost eight hundred miles from what was familiar. It may as well have been one million miles. The one person I could call anytime who *always* knew just what to say could barely speak above a whisper and happened to be in hospice care actively dying. One by one the crutches were being removed. What I know now that I did not know then is the fact that God was systematically and very strategically establishing in me a testimony.

Growing up with grandparents who were steeped in the faith lent to much counsel, hands-on direction, and above all else, the example of godly lives. They lived what they preached. It is not hard to believe someone who is living proof of what they profess. My grandmother was pregnant with my mother when she received the baptism of the Holy Spirit. They were living in Arkansas at the time, and how they had to move from Arkansas to New York so my mother could meet my father is a very interesting story.

My mother, the seventh of nine children, was born in the seventh month in the year of 1957. She later met my father, who happened to be the seventh of eleven children, the sixth son, born in 1956. They ended up being high school sweethearts. As it goes, boy meets girl, they fall in love, and before you know it, here comes 1974. It's a new year and it introduces a new bouncing baby boy. It's a new year that presents new challenges.

There are no coincidences in God.

Life in New York State was much different from what these native Southerners were accustomed to, but the adjustments were welcomed. Little did any of us know that I would, years later, be making the same move in the opposite direction for the same reason, the pursuit of a better life.

Let's rewind. Shortly after my mother was born, my grandfather accepted his call to the ministry. The entire family was at that very moment set on a new course and a new trajectory. Before he began pastoring, they were thrust into the throws of church work. They were no strangers to hard work nor to building a church. In 1970 he accepted his initial pastoral assignment at the Cornerstone #2 Church of God in Christ in Lockport, New York. In 1971 he launched the Sanctuary of God Church of God in Christ in Buffalo, New York. In 1974 this young pastor had to figure out how to deal with the first of his own children, his unmarried teenage daughter, being pregnant. You will have to remember the church was not as liberal then as it is today. That was during the time in Holiness churches when individuals found in this predicament were forced to stand in front of the congregation and confess their sins in hopes of being forgiven and restored to fellowship. Though it was the order of the day, it was nothing that Elder Solomon ever subscribed to. I have heard countless individuals all my life who have referred to him as having the right name. He truly was a wise man. He handled this situation with the same grace that he extended to others in their situations. It was only a matter of time before my parents were united in holy matrimony. Of all the possible outcomes, the one that was divinely orchestrated is the outcome that prevailed.

By the time I came along, firstborn child to the seven, grandchild number three, the church had been established. Family dynamics had changed. The last of my parents' siblings had been born. The tide was about to turn once again. Things were coming together. What could have been an ugly situation in the eyes of man (especially church folks) was really a blessing in disguise. Had it not been handled properly, it would have set off a riptide of negative aftereffects. Thank God for a man of God who could hear from God.

The instructions my grandfather gave to my father were, "Bring the child to me. When you're ready to support a family, you can have him back." In the meantime, and even after going to live with my parents, I spent quite a bit of time under the tutelage of a master teacher who also happened to be a husband, a father, a grandfather, a mentor, a counselor, and a pastor. I cannot forget that in all of this, he also was a man of integrity. He kept his word.

And he removed from thence, and digged another well; and for that they strove not: and he called the name of it Rehoboth; and he said, For now the L*ord* *hath made room for us, and we shall be fruitful in the land.*
(Genesis 26:22)

It is simply amazing how God will use what looks like a mistake and prove to the whole world that it is really a miracle. Learning how to adapt and overcome is a sure sign of wisdom. It is the hallmark of maturity. One word spoken out of season can disrupt the whole course of nature and set ablaze many forests. But a word of wisdom spoken in love can build many nations. Like He did with Isaac, who had to overcome much discomfort from dealing people who did not want him to succeed, carved out space especially for him and his good attitude about it all, "*And he removed from thence, and digged another well; and for that they strove not: and he called the name of it Rehoboth; and he said, For now the* L*ord* *hath made room for us, and we shall be fruitful in the land*" (Gen. 26:22). Alas, the Lord made room for us.

My grooming for ministry began at a very early age. By the time I was ten, I had done more in the church than many five times my senior. I was still very young when I realized that I was different. There were many things I simply was not allowed to do. There were also certain activities I was not allowed to engage in. Most of the time, I felt that I was being punished and that my youth was stolen from me. "*When I was a child, I spake as a child, I understood as a child, I thought as a child: but when I became a man, I put away childish things*" (1 Cor. 13:11). Growing pangs are very real. They are part of the process of becoming. Becoming who we are created to be means that at some point we must abandon whatever inhibitions we may have of who we should be, in order to embrace the possibilities of who we can be. Who we think we should be looms in comparison to who God sees us to be. Change is necessary to the cycle of life. Change is inevitable, and change can be good whether it is welcome or not.

My dad, whom I generally refer to as "my hero," has in recent years finally shared with me his story. It has helped me immensely. There was so much that I had assumed and so much that did not make sense about me until he offered the missing pieces. Just a few weeks ago he said to me, "Hey, son, see how all this has worked out? Now it's our time. Your grandfather did his part. I didn't understand it then, and there were many days I was angry because I felt like he thought I was incompetent. The truth is, he was looking at you from a totally different view. That was a wise old man." Though he was always present, we have not always been closely connected. In Ecclesiastes King Solomon says, "*To every thing there is a season, and a time to every purpose under the heaven*" (Eccl. 3:1).

I will never forget the parting words of my grandfather, and the only pastor I had known up to that point in my life, on the day I went to talk to him about my final decision of relocating to Charlotte, North Carolina. See, I had reluctantly accepted the offer from a major firm that was expanding its footprint. I sat across the room in his study, shaking like a leaf and stammering as I pleaded my case. It was a very lucrative offer and the chance to move my new bride to a more promising city. He calmly said to me after a long, awkward pause, "Son, if the only reason I had to start Sanctuary of God was to prepare you for ministry, I have fulfilled my purpose. From this ministry, greatness has been birthed." He released me with his blessing. What a relief! God knew that without my pastor's blessing, I would have never left. It was time. He knew it and I knew it.

But one thing he knew that I did not was his health status. Looking back now, I believe I understand why he did not share that information with me. It also happened to be the last time I would hear him speak to me in full voice and strength.

Welcome to Charlotte, North Carolina!

Or as my new pastor would say, "Welcome to God's country." We came in, rolled up our sleeves, and as I had done all my life, got to work. The transition was much easier than I anticipated. The only blood family we had here ended up staying only long enough to help us get situated. Only a few months after our arrival, they moved back to Buffalo to start over. God's plan began to rapidly unfold. When I say everything that I was familiar with was a thing of the past, I mean everything! In an aha moment, I shared with my wife this thought: "Well, baby girl, we are about to find out how real our faith in God is." No truer words have ever been spoken. I am eternally grateful for her response: "I trust you. I know you hear from God."

Diamonds are made under extreme pressure. Silver and gold get their shine only after experiencing intense heat, and all precious stones are polished before presentment. Ready or not, here it comes! This "it" was heat, pressure, and buffing. It was, for the lack of a better word, a Job-like experience brewing. These twenty-five years of marriage have proofed many of the nuptial vows we took that beautiful sunshiny June day. To God be the glory for the things He has done.

Five

Testing Time

Wherefore the rather, brethren,
give diligence to make your calling and election sure:
for if ye do these things, ye shall never fall.
(2 Peter 1:10)

When you encounter your strength, embrace it. Embrace it immediately and be about the business of becoming better acquainted with it. There was a time when I was thoroughly convinced, and was even persuaded in my own mind, that I knew what tests and trials were. However, God seemingly has a way of revealing Himself amid adversity. In my experience, it has mostly been through the means of self-discovery. It is not until we are buffeted that we find what is below the surface.

The last time I picked up a pen to make an entry to this collection of thoughts was many years ago. My son was five and my daughter was three. As you can imagine, much about where I was then is very different from where I am now. I'm still wrapping my head around the fact that Junior is twenty-three and Princess is twenty, and neither of them was born when this journal began. It was 1992, and I was a recent high school graduate entering freshman year at St. Bonaventure University; I had not even met my wife yet. It was not until 2023 that the urge to tell my story became so pressing. In May of 2023, I ran across a box that had never been unpacked from our most recent move from South Carolina to North Carolina. I did not bother to open it because I'm a creature of habit and *everything* is clearly labeled with markers. Since I already knew what was in the box marked "Journals," there was no need to open it. Besides, my bookshelves were full.

For whatever reason, I felt compelled to look through it that day. Just as I remembered, there were the seventy-six journals that I had collected and logged in to since elementary school. It was quite interesting to see how my penmanship had changed over the years, but even more interesting to me was to see that they were not in their usual sequential order. That immediately arrested my attention. On the top of the collection was the journal I began the day that I checked in at St. Bonaventure University as an eager freshman. I recorded the whole day. The third night on campus I had a dream. It was so significant that I wrote down as many details as I could remember when I woke up.

In this dream, I was standing in the middle of the street of an old neighborhood I'd grown up in near Buffalo, New York. It was daylight and the sky was clear. As I looked up, an angel appeared and told me there were four dates that I should remember. They were June 10, May 25, July 18, and March 31. The journal entry was dated 10/28/1992 @ 6:42 a.m. Since that time, all these dates have resurfaced in many ways, both prominent and significant ways.

My son's due date was projected to be June 10, 2000. He was born April 1, 2000, weighing 2 lbs., 0 oz. He was kept in the neonatal intensive care unit (NICU) of the hospital until he could finish developing and we were able to take him home. This child, whom the doctors had given a 50 percent chance to live, was now healthy and ready to come home. Hallelujah! We were at the hospital daily from April 1 to June 10. The entire time, I managed to work a full-time, forty-hours-a-week corporate job and not miss a single ministry assignment.

An hour after getting our little bundle of joy settled into his new crib, our excitement was silenced by a phone call announcing the passing of my maternal grandfather. What next? Well, next was the discovery of new strength. It became more apparent than ever that faith in God had to be more than a notion. All my life up until then, I'd had a hands-on counselor and a real-life coach.

And Saul armed David with his armour, and he put an helmet of brass upon his head; also he armed him with a coat of mail. And David girded his sword upon his armour, and he assayed to go; for he had not proved it. And David said unto Saul, I cannot go with these; for I have not proved them. And David put them off him.
(1 Samuel 17:38–39)

Looking back, I can see in hindsight what I was being prepared for. Knowing that then (if it were possible) would not have been welcomed news. I do not know a living soul who would have gladly walked into the blows I was about to be dealt.

On March 31, 2013, our lives were forever changed. After numerous doctors' visits and several misdiagnoses came the hard news of the "big C." My eldest child, who had already had such a difficult premature birth, was now being challenged with another major life-threatening event. How does a parent appropriately respond to a child who is looking into their eyes and asking, "What did I do wrong to make this happen to me?" I felt as if all the air had been sucked out of the room. We had way more questions than they had answers. I felt as though that day was longer than twenty-four hours for some reason. Thank God for a pediatrician who was insistent that we not be brushed off again.

This was the first doctor's appointment that my wife insisted that I be present for. Typically, as a stay-at-home mom, she handled all the things with the children that happened during my normal work hours. At this point, she was not satisfied with the care my son was getting. None of the trial medications or treatments been effective, nor had the diagnoses accurate, so she'd asked me to take the day off and make sure we were heard. Our son was experiencing fainting spells that were becoming increasingly more frequent. We were aware of two small knots on his neck that apparently had been moving around. We were initially told it was a minor allergic reaction; he was given Benadryl, and it was suggested to us to change our laundry detergent and soap. On this visit with his primary care physician, a full examination was performed. That is when we were made aware of the other lumps on his body more than the two we saw. Our son had never complained of the pain nor the multiple knots because he didn't want to bother us. *What?!* You would just have to know his personality.

His pediatrician made a referral to the children's specialty hospital an hour and a half away. They told her he could be seen in two months. When she said, "No, he must be seen today!" we knew something serious was going on. We had to remain collected. Less than fifty feet away was the school our children attended, so we picked up our daughter and got on the road. Upon our arrival, we were met at the door by a team of medical professionals. The head physician came in on his day off. It was like a whirlwind. Everything was happening so fast. The specialist knew within the first ten minutes of his probe what was going on. Driving home was like walking the green mile. No one knew what to say. We were processing it all, each in our own way. The next day would be our son's thirteenth birthday. Instead of a party, we were packing up to begin what would end up being a two-year journey.

From April 2013 to July 2015, we spent more than 340 nights away from home. That included hospital stays, the Ronald McDonald House, and rehabilitation centers. In the process of time, our son received the maximum allowable amount of chemotherapy and radiation. He experienced 100 percent kidney failure, dialysis, and several surgeries. After all of that, we were told that nothing was working. He had not only the rarest form of leukemia (ALL, Type T), but it was compromised with a Philadelphia chromosome. The doctors were stumped. Nothing was working. To further complicate things, he was severely constipated from a combination of the medication and the treatments and had been unable to urinate for a couple of days. When the nurse came in to give him a fourth dose of whatever it was to assist flushing him out, he said to her that it was not working and was making things worse. She told him he had to take it, doctor's orders. He looked at me and said, "Daddy, please don't let them make me keep taking that; it's making me sicker." I looked at the nurse and said, "He will not be taking any more of that." She replied, "I'm sorry, Mr. Samuel; he does not have a choice." I said to her, "Oh, there's always a choice, and we choose to refuse to continue with this medication. Thank you."

Soon after, on that beautiful spring day, the dedicated medical team stopped in the room for their daily update. The lead doctor began his update with a question: "Do you have a prayer group at your church?" I thought that was a very unusual question, but I told him yes. He proceeded to say, "This will be the time to reach out to them for support." That feeling from March 31, 2013, started resurfacing. Then he said, "Do you have adequate burial insurance? All we can do now is make him comfortable. We've done all we can do. It's in God's hands."

I begged pardon and asked my wife to take our daughter to the cafeteria. The nurses started crying, and the physician assistants were misty-eyed, taking notes and passing around a box of Kleenex. I switched positions from the bench with the doctor to a chair next to my son's bed. Somehow Junior had taken great interest in whatever was on the television. The doctor stood up and asked that Junior mute the television. He muted it, but he remained fixated on the screen. The doctor stood at the foot of the bed and said, "Junior, do you understand what is going on?" My son lowered his hand holding the remote, looked at the doctor, and said, "Anything you want me to know, tell my parents and they will explain it to me." He proceeded to lift the remote back up and laugh. The doctor looked at me. I looked at Junior, who was totally unbothered, looked back at the doctor, and shrugged my shoulders. As I held my son's hand, the peace that he was experiencing came over me.

The doctor said, "Junior, we just want you to be prepared and understand that you will not be attending your prom or graduating from high school. Do you understand that you will never have children?" It was at that point that the faith shift happened. My son turned his face toward me and said, "Hey, Dad, what do you want me to name your first grandchild?"

I almost hollered! The doctor gathered his staff and asked them to be sure they documented everything. His recommendation was that a psychological evaluation be performed. This same doctor, who moments earlier had asked if our church had a prayer team, on his way out of the door looked back to say to me how unfortunate it was that my beliefs had transferred to my children. "This never turns out good," he said. That was my cue to stand up. I told the doctor we would not be accepting any further recommendations for treatment from him. I thanked him for his services. His response to me was "I hope you realize you just signed his death certificate," and completed his exit. How arrogant was that?

When my wife and daughter returned to the room, my wife asked, "How did things go?" I said, "Exactly the way they were supposed to." I left to go over to the church, which was about seven minutes away, for prayer. I needed some quiet time to gather myself and to hear from God. Upon my arrival at the church, I found a few of the church mothers preparing to leave. They had felt led to come over to the church to pray for Junior and our family. I was humbled. Apparently, they had been doing that periodically for some time, but I did not know about it. Of course, they wanted to know what was going on and what the doctors were saying since their last update.

As I began to share, they were stirred with righteous indignation. "Who does he think he is? He's not God. God has the final say!" One of the mothers said to me, "Listen, Sam, this is what you need to do. Get that baby some prune juice. Warm it like you would hot tea and let him sip it." I said, "Yes, ma'am." The funny thing is, my children actually loved prune juice, though we had never drunk it warm before. At this point, I was willing to try anything other than what they were experimenting with in the hospital. Needless to say, I forgot what I went to the church for. I left with those ladies and went straight to the grocery store and right back to the hospital.

When I got to the room, I noticed that they had disconnected all the IVs. Junior was just lying there, quietly watching television. I started to ask, but I didn't. I told him I had brought him something that mothers at the church wanted him to try and that it would make him feel better. He said, "Okay." I fixed the juice as I had been instructed. About halfway through, Junior jumped up to run to the bathroom. He had a mighty deliverance. We clapped and cheered just as we did when he learned how to use the potty alone at two years old. Look at God!

That night I stayed, and Catherine went to the Ronald McDonald House so she could get in the bed and try to have a good night's rest. We were going to be trading places the next day; my leave of absence from my job had expired. I remember praying all night. I was pleading with God for direction and asking if I had made a mistake with taking that stance with the medical staff. I had ordered the suspension of all medication, and they were threatening neglect of a minor, *God, I need an answer!*

While I was praying, I was also preparing notes for the sermon I would be preaching that week. I ran across a phrase that apparently I had missed all the years I had read it. This time the words jumped off the page at me: *"Wherefore, sirs, be of good cheer: for* I believe God, *that it shall be even as it was told me"* (Acts 27:25, emphasis added). There was a promise that God made to the apostle Paul when he attempted to warn the seamen that traveling would not be wise with the pending climactic changes. They ended up shipwrecked. Though those in charge would not listen, God maintained what he had promised Paul, that none would perish. Some survived on broken pieces, some swam to shore, and the rest made it on boards. It was rough, but they made it.

The next morning, just before I had to leave to get to work on time, we were introduced to a bright young doctor new to the staff, who had just been assigned to Junior as his new doctor. His bedside manner was impeccable. He took time to explain to us that he had spent time reading our son's charts. He disagreed with much of what the previous physician had chosen as treatment, particularly the aggressive radiation treatments. He asked if we would trust him to come up with an alternate plan of treatment to save our son's life. I told him he was the answer to our prayers. He told me he didn't believe in God, but he would not knock our faith.

He had been placed in charge of a new unit. We were one of sixteen families under his care in this special unit. There were eight rooms on each corridor, with a nurses' station in the center on both sides. Behind each nurses' station were two rooms with double doors. The four children with the most severe cases occupied those rooms. Junior was one of them. Over the course of the next thirteen months, we saw the lights go out one by one. The patients in the room next to Junior's behind the nurses' station changed three times. I remember, the first night we heard "Code Blue" and saw the flashing lights, asking the nurse, "What does that mean?" The answer, I will never forget. All the parents, each time did whatever we could to console one another. We watched the double corridor of rooms dwindle to only one side being used. We saw how the staff was consolidated, and patients were moved closer and closer together. Eventually, the only two rooms in the entire unit that were being used were right behind the nurses' station. Late one night we were awakened by the flashing lights followed by the haunting sound of "Code Blue." We slowly stepped out into the hallway to see if we could offer some comfort to our friendly neighbors that we had kind of gotten attached to over the past several weeks. Before I could say anything, the distraught mother looked at me and said, "What's so special about your kid that he gets to live and mine doesn't?" I was stunned and completely lost for words. I said to the father that we would pray for them, as we had said to each other daily until that day. He replied, "Save those prayers for your own kid. He'll need them—he's next."

Fifteen out of sixteen children treated in that unit were now deceased. Junior was the sole survivor. The staff mustered every ounce of energy, love, and care they could into doing whatever they could for the one child who was left. Everything the new doctor prepared us for, we received the opposite results. When he told us our son's hair would fall out, it grew thicker. He said his skin would darken, but it lightened. They told us his growth would be stunted, but he had a spurt. They said the treatments would block the normal progression of pubescence, but it did not. What caught everyone by surprise was kidney failure and the loss of his ability to walk.

Once his kidneys were restored, we were told that he would probably end up in a wheelchair, but that hard news would be the better alternative, since he would still be with us a little longer. Every once in a while, we replay the videos that we'd captured on our mobile phones of him learning how to walk again in two-thirds of the time they'd said would be the minimum time for him to regain the necessary strength and mobility. When he was admitted to the rehabilitation facility, he told the nurse when he was going home. She told him that date was quite hopeful but just not possible. She went on to say that it was the same amount of time for everyone; in fact, twenty-one days was the minimum, and though some ended up staying longer no one ever stayed shorter. Junior repeated to her the day he would be going home. The nurse went and got her pocket planner and marked the day Junior said he was going home. They both initialed it, and she told the whole staff. They thought it was cute. I also took notes because this little guy had been teaching us lessons in faith that I had not believed were possible.

Fourteen days after his entry into the rehab, the very date that Junior said it would be, we were going home. We bypassed the Ronald McDonald House and the hospital. Both places were prepared to accommodate us. As we were packing to leave, the doctors, therapists, and nurses took turns coming to look at the miracle. Every one of them said, either coming or going, "This is *amazing!*" I never heard one word so many times on the same day. They were speaking to not only his progress from his time at the rehab, but his overall recovery and defying the odds—all the odds.

Miracle at 8065—

We were in the home stretch when my wife had taken ill. There was a time I was splitting my time between the two of them on different floors in the same hospital. By the end of 2014, I'd decided there were changes I needed to make if I was going to live to be any good to anyone else. I made the decision to have weight loss surgery. It happened in January 2015, and in good time. I was able to schedule my operations between my son having complications and having major surgery. I lost 140 pounds. Things were looking up. On Sunday, March 8, 2015, I was appointed as interim pastor at the Historic Sherman Memorial COGIC. On Tuesday, March 31, 2015, I was doing a bone marrow transplant for my son.

After all the advancements we had made and as bright as things were looking, our new doctor said he had exhausted every method he knew. There was only one more option left to eradicate the remaining cancer cells, but it would be risky. Of the millions of donors in the database, there was not a single match. We sampled more than fifty relatives and dozens of church members and friends, but no, not one. The doctor came back and said there was one thing we could try. He said, "At 50 percent, Mr. Samuel, you are the closest match. Stem cell transplanting is new, and we don't have much data, but I think it's worth a try." It worked. The doctor who had said he did not believe in God when he announced to us that he was offered a position at Johns Hopkins Hospital but was committed to following Junior the rest of his life, now said, "Y'all have caused me to reconsider." He concluded that conversation by letting us know that a private anonymous donor had covered all our outstanding medical debts. They committed to covering all future indebtedness related to Junior's aftercare, and they would be following Junior for the rest of his life as well and monitoring his progress. Roughly $312,000 was wiped out just like that.

This is why I *BELIEVE* GOD!

Six

Called. Equipped. Sent.

Moreover whom he did predestinate, them he also called: and whom he called, them he also justified: and whom he justified, them he also glorified.
(Romans 8:30)

We have made so many celebrities, super-saints, and untouchables in Christianity today that it's simply ridiculous. At the same time, we have seen so many make such a spectacle and complete mockery of the church of Christ that it is nothing short of a miracle that the world has any remaining respect for the church.

The most memorable sermon I remember hearing my grandfather preach was seared in my memory because of the illustration he used to close it out. The text he took was Matthew 22:14: *"For many are called, but few are chosen."* He took his time, as was his custom, to masterfully explain the scripture contextually then seal the lesson with an example of how to use the information practically. He would often say his job as teacher was to make it make sense to the student, humbly asking, "Lord, help me to make it so plain that a fool won't err."

The illustrations he used were always actual events, and most times those events had occurred right in our faces. He took full advantage of breaking down the obvious and helping us get a different perspective. The analogy he chose to bring home the lesson for us this particular week was about my aunt. She was the youngest of his children and just six years my senior. We were very close growing up, almost like siblings. Though she and I were close in age, I was taught, as a sign of respect, to always address her as "Aunt Tracy," just as I addressed the other aunts and uncles in our sprawling family.

One day my grandmother, while preparing supper, realized that she didn't have all the ingredients she needed to finish, so she called out for Aunt Tracy to go to the store for her to pick up what was missing. I was "not old enough to go alone," or so I was told (though the store was less than a block away). At the time that Grandmother called for Aunt Tracy, only one of them understood why she was called.

When Aunt Tracy heard the voice, she ran toward it. By the time she came downstairs and stood before Grandmother, she was still excited about being called, excited because she knew she was called for a reason. Now she was standing before the one who had called her. Grandmother said to her, "I want you to go to the store for me." An Aunt Tracy just took off running. She ran right through the house, out the door, up the street, and all the way to the store. My grandmother looked over at me and said, "*Well, sir. . . .* " I just shrugged my shoulders. My grandfather laughed. No one moved. A few minutes later the young, enthusiastic runner was reentering the house with a slow walk of shame. She had left the house without her assignment, without instructions, and without being empowered with the bartering tools she needed to complete the task.

Here comes the great sermon close Elder Solomon used that fateful Sunday:

> People of God, we must understand that being sent is a process. You cannot skip steps and still get the desired results. Understand that there is a difference between being called and being sent. Many are called, but the sent have submitted to the process of becoming who God has called them to be. In other words, the Father calls us away from where we are to another place in order to give us instructions and to equip us for where He is sending us to. We cannot afford to be in such a hurry to get to the sending that we miss the steps. Missing steps, missteps,

are why we see so many fallen leaders today. There are so many who have fallen because they have been exposed to ministry assignments prematurely. It is not because they were not called; it is because they did not wait. It is because they did not submit to the process of becoming who God was calling them to be.

Through waiting the second time around, Aunt Tracy was able to respond to the call appropriately. That meant standing before the one who called, receiving the necessary instructions (in this instance, a grocery list), and getting enough money to purchase everything on the list. Then came the charge: "Go! And don't forget to bring back my change."

Once you have been properly released to go by the one who has the authority to send you, then and only then are you legitimately going as an ambassador. Ambassadors represent the interests of others. They are authorized agents. As ambassadors of Christ, we are fully vetted and fully covered. Learning to focus on what is most important is the best way to avoid much confusion and unnecessary frustration.

We have seen so many who started out strong in their ministry and finished weak. Very few are willing to endure shame, scandal, or embarrassment. It is much easier to hide or find an alternate route of escape from a proverbial stoning than it is to stand and take the hits, especially not knowing if the fatal rock is in the pile. Not all growth is healthy. Infectious swelling is growth, while healthy growth is sustainable growth. Healthy growth is typically slow and gradual but lasting. Before there can be fruit, a seed must be planted. That seed must go through the stages of germination. Germination in itself is a process. Submit to it. What is germination? It is what happens when a seed is planted in soil. The work that goes on out of sight includes the seed expanding to release what is inside of it. The outer layers are broken off.

Repetition is the mother of retention.

Taking into consideration the training I received over the years, I am now aware of the purpose of many of those lessons. It is not very often that we immediately use the bulk of what we learn on a day-to-day basis. I have asked God to increase my storehouse capacity. Scientists say that we lose 80 percent of what we hear and fully comprehend within hours of having heard it. Retention then is the challenge. It is not "getting" it; it's "keeping what we got."

So then faith cometh by hearing, and hearing by the word of God.
(Romans 10:17)

Hearing and hearing! Faith comes as a result of remaining connected and open. When I worked in banking, I had this saying posted on the wall in my cubicle: "Knowledge is power. Get all the power you can." Many days it served as a reminder to me that I was responsible for my personal growth. Isaiah 55:10 says that God gives *"seed to the sower, and bread to the eater."* That gives me to know that God is interested in blessing those with a work ethic and those with an appetite. It is my sincere desire to be that guy who has worked hard enough to have worked up an appetite.

Being authorized by God as a laborer in His fields means that you have successfully completed the process of being sent.

Step 1: **Called.** The day you hear His voice, receive it with a glad heart remember that many are called, but few are chosen. The chosen are those who have decided that following Christ is worth bearing the cross that comes with His calling. The chosen answer the call. Not everyone called responds properly. There's always a choice. Choosing right is up to the individual. Our certification is validated by our obedience to His word.

Step 2: **Equipped.** This is the most crucial part of the process, as it is the growth and development phase. This is where the rubber meets the road.

Being equipped or armed with the necessary tools to finish the assignment successfully requires time. Unfortunately, we cannot skip steps in the process and still get the desired results. Learning takes time. It requires discipline and conditioning. In order to be skillful with the tools needed for any job, understanding as much as possible about those tools is essential.

Wherefore the rather, brethren, give diligence to make your calling and election sure: for if ye do these things, ye shall never fall.
(2 Peter 1:10)

Step 3: **Sent.** Being sent is not guaranteed to everyone who is called. Your gift will make room for you; it will get you to where you need to go, but your character is what gets you a seat and keeps you there. If we look at how Jesus handled the disciples, we see a clear picture of the process of being sent. His selection of the Twelve demonstrates winning characteristics. They were all working already. They were individuals, uniquely gifted.

The call is made to arrest our attention. It is a summons to come in for instruction and connection. Getting equipped is preparation for practice. There were two things I heard my grandfather say often when I was growing up that were against the norm. The first was contradictory of the old saying "Practice makes perfect." He believed that practicing *right* makes perfect. He often cautioned me, "Son, you can be sincere and sincerely wrong at the same time." The second was in response to folks saying, "One monkey doesn't stop the show." He'd say, "Well, that's not entirely true. It depends on which monkey it is." There are certain prerequisites to becoming a practitioner. Understand that a practitioner is one who would be considered an expert in their profession, a trusted professional.

All craftsmen have tools for their trade. They are experts only in their fields of study. In other words, lawyers need doctors, doctors need restauranteurs, and they all need mechanics. When it comes to a world that is seeking answers or an experience better than what it knows, looking to the church should be both welcomed and rewarding. Being skilled in the

Word of God should be a high priority for every minister. By *minister* I am not just speaking in regard to those who stand behind a podium with a microphone in hand. Rather, I am referring to anyone who serves in any capacity of Christian duty.

> *Therefore said he unto them, The harvest truly is great,*
> *but the labourers are few: pray ye therefore the Lord of the harvest,*
> *that he would send forth labourers into his harvest.*
> (Luke 10:2)

Laborers . . . workmen . . . those who will get the work done without injuring the harvest—that is whom the Lord of the harvest is looking for.

Appointment @ 1401—

The journey to the pastorate of an established church was complicated for me. It was never in my purview. Although I heard it more times than I could count, it was the "how it could ever materialize" that prevented me from ever getting a notion. There had never been a doubt in my mind that I was supposed to be there, but I worked very well in mostly behind-the-scenes capacities.

Upon arriving at Charlotte, North Carolina, there were a few things, in no particular order, that I considered as high priorities if we were going to flourish in our new city: (1) a safe place for my wife and me to live, (2) gainful employment commensurate to my skill set, and (3) a church where I could be planted and grow. The Lord blessed us with all three immediately. What more could I ask for?

We were received with open arms. It was not long at all before we found an area in the church to work in. We were glad to do it. Eventually, I was the number two man. I was like a sponge soaking up all the wisdom I could. I had no idea that it was all preparation for today. Like David, I have experienced three anointings.

Seven

The Cost of Greatness

I returned, and saw under the sun, that the race is not to the swift,
nor the battle to the strong,
neither yet bread to the wise, nor yet riches to men of understanding,
nor yet favour to men of skill;
but time and chance happeneth to them all.
(Ecclesiastes 9:11)

Our God is faithful!

The greatest miracles happen in the dark, behind the scenes, and sometimes right in the dirt. I'm totally convinced of it. Though science has been able to explain the phenomenon of human birth and the process of plant growth from seed to tree, there yet remains a mystery that cannot be articulated or defined. That is why some achieve certain things in life and others do not. There are as many theories on that as there are winners and losers in the world.

However, there is much to be said of individuals who have worked their way up through the ranks. David is a prime example of one who waited on his time to shine. He was anointed to be king way before a public coronation. In fact, his first anointing was quiet, unassuming, and very private. The second was a trial run and test of endurance, but his third anointing was his official induction to the annals of time and the beginning of his historic reign.

David is that single person in Scripture whose life was so multifaceted and tiered that just about any of us could find ourselves having similarities in different phases of his life—from being the most unlikely candidate for promotion, to being guilty of seeing others' flaws and not one's own, to being eaten up with guilt for having done things that we could have avoided. David's life was on full display, live and in living color. Though he has been dead and gone for a long time, we are still talking about what he did. Though we can all benefit from his story, its creation came at a high price.

If the oil was for everyone, it wouldn't hold its value.

It comes at a price not everyone can afford. Okay, I will say it another way: greatness comes at a cost not everyone is willing to pay. Whether we refer to it as greatness or the anointing, either way know this: it ain't cheap! If anyone could be you, why aren't they? Being different is a lonely place, but being different is rewarding. Being different is the vehicle God chose to get you to your next. His hand is on your life, but He never forces the direction you take. He will only influence when *you* listen. The choice to obey is always up to you. Choosing wisely, choosing right, choosing Him releases the oil. The anointing is God's approval and authorization that allows you to function effectively in whatever role or responsibilities you've been called to undertake.

The cost of admission to the realm of greatness is survivorship—*Live!* The membership fee is persistence— *Don't Give Up!* Consistency is the price to pay for longevity. Greatness does not wear off. It does not expire. It is the stuff that legacies are made of. The fact that you made it, of the millions of seeds released at conception, says that you are strong. It says you have purpose.

From the limited knowledge I have about reproduction; I have read that the phenomenon of twins occurs somewhere around 3 percent of all births in the United States annually. That is a very small percentage in comparison to the grand scheme of things. Since I do not believe there are coincidences in God, I find it very interesting that both my maternal grandmother, Lula Mae Solomon, and my fraternal grandmother, Lila Mae Samuel, married men who were born as a twin. I've always been fascinated with twins, especially identical twins. I was not blessed to produce any myself, but in 2018 at a church leadership conference in Atlanta, Georgia, I met a man whose path to the pastorate was so similar to mine that the story is too good to leave out. Remember, there are no coincidences in God.

On the first night of the conference, I was so tired. We had driven from Charlotte to Atlanta. It is only about a four-hour drive, but I had not rested prior to getting on the road. When we arrived, we registered for the sessions, checked into our rooms, and hit the ground running. By that evening, when it was time for the general session, I was wiped out. I decided that I would sleep in and have a fresh start the next morning. Everyone had gone down for service. I could not sleep. I felt a strong pull to get up, get dressed, and be there in person. I was watching the service via live stream but still felt compelled to go. Eventually, I made my way to the ballroom. The place was packed. I stood at the door, scoping out somewhere to sit. I texted everyone I knew who was there, asking where they were sitting and if there was an open seat. No one responded. Just when I started to turn around and go back upstairs, I saw a row with two empty seats near the aisle (great view to the stage, by the way). As I approached the seats, I asked those in the immediate vicinity if they were taken. Everyone said no. By the time I was situated, it was time for the evening speaker to take the floor. When he mounted the podium, he began his message by asking us to take a good look around and see who was sitting in front, on either side, and behind us. He proceeded to say that he sat and watched us coming in while he was awaiting his time to speak. "Most of you looked at the chair you would occupy but didn't look or speak to the persons near it." That comment sparked a lot of chuckles. He said, "No, that really isn't funny. It's an indictment." He went on to say, "There were very few of you who greeted the persons in the area around you before taking a seat. I wonder how many pastors here know that the members in your churches are the same way?"

A huge buzz was going on at this point. He had arrested the attention of the audience. We all wanted to know where he was going with it. He then asked, "This is a leadership conference, is it not?" In choir-like synchrony, there was a reverberating Yes. He said, "Please do me a favor. Take your time and introduce yourself to someone near you. Find out where they are from and what they do. If they are a pastor, get some information about their church. Then I want you to exchange with them your information."

My pew partner was from Houston, Texas. He told me his story first. In 2015 he became pastor of an historic church formerly led by a bishop. He was a son of the church and had left the church that he launched to return home. I started laughing while he was talking. He gave me the strangest look, understandably so, but I was so amused with how he was telling my story. Of all the people I could have ended up sitting next to, it so happened to be someone who has consistently, and as recently as this year, been a voice of encouragement to me from that day to this one. Every time we have communicated, it has been divinely orchestrated. God always knows what we need and when we need it.

Over the years, we have shared with each other some of the challenges we have faced that are unique to pastors who succeed pastors who were "sho nuff" pastors. Trying to step into shoes that you can never fill can be quite intimidating.

It's not revelation until it's revelation to you.

With the discovery that God never intended for any one of us to fill the shoes of another comes not only great liberation, but also an awesome burden. How then shall *you* bear this burden? Here are three points to ponder:

The Cost of Greatness

(1) Know that it is only your burden alone if you are stronger than God, who has called you to it.
(2) Remember that you are uniquely made. Just as there is only one you today, your predecessor was once one of them.
(3) If He called you to it, He knew before you did that you were the one He wanted to do it.

Eight

Dangers of Premature Exposure

Now Moses kept the flock of Jethro his father in law, the priest of Midian: and he led the flock to the backside of the desert, and came to the mountain of God, even to Horeb.
(Exodus 3:1)

The sense of "time's a wastin'" is the very thing that causes so many to move out of sync with destiny. We live in a time when virtually everything is available immediately. We can even purchase vehicles and have them delivered to our residences without ever leaving the house. Even the convenience of drive-through restaurants has been compromised. Impatient humans become extremely creative in desperate times. The feeling of the clock working against them or time being unfriendly can prompt hasty decisions and poor judgment.

Getting ahead of God is a surefire sign of misdirected trust. Moving too slowly and missing God is just as bad. There is such a great lesson to be learned from Moses's experience on the backside of the desert. It was a place of obscurity, a place of isolation. Many times God will pull us away from everyone and everything to minister to us. He will set us aside where no one but Him has access to us so that He can speak to us. It is in those quiet times that we receive our deepest revelations.

Now, this is where I can share some of what my experience was when I realized that I was right where I was supposed to be. Growing up, I always felt as if home was somewhere else. I was always the oddball—in school, at home, and with people my age. The church was my happy place. It was even better than escaping through a book, which was another guilty pleasure of mine. Don't get me wrong, I was not unhappy as a kid. I just always felt as if there was more than what I knew and where I had been. There was a deep longing to branch out and to see more. I wanted to be part of something bigger than Buffalo. I dreamt about it all the time. When I was not asleep, I was imagining what it would be like not to have to shovel snow again.

Before I knew what a vision board was, I heard an evangelist on the first night of a three-night revival say that God was challenging His people to pray with specificity. The first night, I was with a few friends. It seemed to me that everyone was especially blessed. It was an okay experience for me, but I did not quite feel as though I had gotten what I should have out of the service. The second night, I had to work late and was on the fence with whether or not I would go at all. Though it was late, I decided to get dressed and go anyway. By the time I got there, he had just gotten up to preach. The church was packed. I knew it would be. Both parking lots were full, and I ended up parking a few blocks away and walking.

When I got inside, I looked through the windows of the vestibule trying to find where my friends were sitting, hoping they had saved a seat for me. People were standing in the hallways, listening over the intercom. Some were lined around the walls in the sanctuary. I finally caught the eye of one of my friends. He motioned for me to come on over to where they had been holding a spot for me. The moment I got settled in good, I noticed the preacher had shifted. He stopped almost mid-speech and asked me to stand up. When I stood up, he said, "You're a preacher, aren't you?" Before I could answer, he said, "I know you are. You don't have to answer that. The Holy Ghost told me." At this point, I was beyond nervous. I had been in the church all my life. I had seen all kinds of foolishness. I had no idea where he was going with this . . . in front of all these people.

He told me to lift my hands, so I did. He proceeded to say, "Man of God, I saw you when you walked in here and down the aisle. I see millions of dollars all around you. God is about to fill your pockets." Everyone around me started yelling and cheering. I closed my eyes so that I could focus on what he was saying. He told me to open my eyes and come to where he was. He called me up from the floor to stand in front of him. On my way down the aisle, I took a deep breath. As I was walking toward him, he shouted, "God said get ready to collect what you're owed." Immediately my mind went back to the previous night when he told us to stop praying so many general prayers and to be specific with God. Well, on my way to the service that night, I had prayed, "Lord, if there is a word for me tonight, I want the preacher to call me out and speak it directly to me." When I got to where the preacher was, he told me to lift up my hands again and look into his eyes. Someone had to tell me what happened after that. All I can remember is he reached out to lay his hand on my head while saying, "Receive it!" When I opened my eyes, I was looking up at the ceiling a good distance away from where I had met the preacher. The parts I remember so well are because I've listened to the recording over and over. One of my friends purchased the audiocassette that night and made me a copy that I still have to this day. His words to me were, "This has got to be written on your heart."

So then faith cometh by hearing, and hearing by the word of God.
(Romans 10:17)

The best form of retention is repetition. It is the hearing and hearing of the Word of God that etches it on our hearts. Here's what I have learned about prophecy: God's timing is not the same as ours. For years (after leaving the church that night thinking I was about to be a multimillionaire in the next twenty-four to forty-eight hours), I imagined a myriad of scenarios of how it was going to happen, or even if it had already happened in ways that I had not considered. At this point, I am resolved to believing that it has not happened yet, but it will. When it does, it will be as it was told to me. I believe God.

In the meantime, there is so much growth and preparation that must occur in me as I make ready to receive what is in store. I am reminded of something a dear friend, who is also an author, said to me when I asked him how many books he had sold. His immediate response was, "Why?" I was not ready with an answer, primarily because I had expected him to just tell me the number. He chose to challenge me instead. When I finally came up with an answer, he shot that down too.

I said, "I want to realistically gauge my expectation on sales." He came back with "Okay, tell me this. Why are you writing? To get rich or to be heard?"

I had to think about that for a moment. After I did, I responded with, "I want to be heard. I believe I have a story to tell." I probably should have left it there, especially knowing whom I was talking to, but I didn't. I went on to say, "I just don't know if I will have an audience."

His closing statement went like this: "Then it won't ever be written, and your story will never be told. You can't write and not be present. Until you are present in the moment, it won't happen. And right now, you're not there because you're worried about things that shouldn't even matter." Premature exposure is a killer!

Some things we have to sit in for a while. Some emotions, thoughts, experiences . . . some moments, we have to sit in until we are actually present in them. We have to sit until we can feel what needs to be felt, smell what needs to be smelled, taste what needs to be tasted. "Going there" can't tell "been there" how to get there. Experience is still the best teacher—yes, after all this time, still.

I thought working in the financial industry was it. After all, I was surrounded my millions and billions of dollars daily. I was a money manager. It was not my money; however, I learned one of my most valuable lessons to date: being a good steward is priceless. A steward is one who is responsible for the care of another's goods. There are two things every believer must ever be conscious of: (1) Being used by God is a privilege. (2) Humility is the way up in God.

Whatever you have been called to do won't ever be about you. Knowing this will keep you from being presumptuous and will help to keep you grounded. Leaving familiar territory, a place where I was known and celebrated, and arriving at a place where nobody knew my name or reputation was a humbling experience, but it was a nonfactor. Why? Because I was sent. Everything that has happened in your life up to now was designed to get you to this point. Submitting to the sovereignty of God does not always show immediate results, but it always has deep roots.

How does an inexperienced, unknown twenty-something-year-old show up at an established church and find space to work? *"A man's gift maketh room for him, and bringeth him before great men"* (Prov. 18:16). You don't have to force fit, shove, or manipulate your way when you walk out the steps that God has ordered for your life. So I showed up. I showed up out of obedience to God. I showed up with no agenda. The only expectation I had was to be fed and to work wherever my gifts could be used. When I prayed and asked God to show me where we should go for a church home, I prayed with specificity. It was my desire not to go to a church that was so small that I would not be able to take a break or be missing without it being a major deal. Second, I did not desire to go to a church so large that the pastor would not know us or was not accessible. I got everything I asked for and more.

This is a bishop's church!

That is a phrase I have heard repeated more times than I can ever count, from my first visit to the Historic Sherman Memorial Church of God in Christ in 1999 to this day. Over the years, I have actually found out what that means. To my surprise, it is not what I thought it meant. From 1970 to 2015, only bishops had served as pastors at this church. The logical conclusion that I had drawn was it was a bishop's church because only bishops had pastored it. Fast-forward to 2023, and it's still a bishop's church, although its current pastor is not a bishop. So then, what does being a bishop's church mean? It means that a standard of excellence has been set, and it is up to all those who remain and those who come up to follow the precedent. That does not mean things won't change or shouldn't, but it does mean that whatever changes are made should enhance and not tarnish.

A bishop's church is a flagship church, one that others will model themselves after. We have been an example to others even without realizing it. Consistency is our friend. Remaining faithful is easy when rough patches are short-term and the rest of life is incident-free. Being faithful during trying times, coming through with victory, living to tell the story is weighty. It's what others need to hear when they're wondering if survival is possible. Steadfastness is a learned behavior, an acquired skill. It does not happen without resistance.

The transition of leadership is momentous for any church or organization. Yet, just as with any other institution, if a church is stable enough, it will outlive not only its founder, but many if not all of his successors. With every new leader comes new territory to conquer, new discoveries to be made, new levels to attain, and new strength to gain. The congregation that I serve has experienced, since its inception, the changing of the guards three times. With each shift also came new workers, but the pillars of this group have helped to stabilize us through the ebbs and flows.

It may not be a church that you are called to serve or protect per se, but you will always have your personal ministry to preserve. The worst thing that can happen to a caterpillar going through the process of metamorphosis to become a butterfly is for its cocoon to be disturbed or broken externally. The last stages of an emerging butterfly are to strengthen its wings by using them to break out of the cocoon. Many have been corrupted and many assignments have been aborted by individuals who thought they were helping someone else by pushing them or trying to make destiny manifest. Know this: there is nothing new under the sun. Nations have been destroyed because of human intervention that prevented nature from running its course.

Waiting is not always the easiest thing to do, but it can prevent a great deal of calamity and the need for a do- over. Biding your time will help to ensure that when it is time to be presented, you will be ready. Timing is everything! God has people, right now, in your life who weren't even born yet when your journey began but are today instrumental to where you are going. He has others who are on their way to where you are but can't get there until they achieve certain milestones in their lives that lead up to their relocation. Any move out of sync affects the next. Be patient! Things are as they should be. Otherwise, they'd be something else. You must believe the Word of God: "*And we know that all things work together for good to them that love God, to them who are the called according to his purpose*" (Rom. 8:28).

There will always be great individuals, but they will never be great alone. Greatness is substantiated by the support it receives. What's feeding you?

NINE

Silence is Consent . . . But to What?

For though ye have ten thousand instructors in Christ, yet have ye not many fathers: for in Christ Jesus, I have begotten you through the gospel.
(1 Corinthians 4:15)

Did I mention that I have two children? In addition to being a "Senior," I have the awesome privilege of being a girl dad too. My daughter is the polar opposite of her older brother. She came after his premature birth but has heard about it all her life. He did not go through his bout with cancer alone. The whole family went through that life-altering ordeal together. Let me tell you what happened to the youngest, the one who was born *after* the doctors told us that our chance of ever having a successful pregnancy was less than 5 percent. I was so happy that the Lord had blessed us with one that I was prepared for an only-child situation. Though Denae was a surprise to me, she was not to my wife. My wife later shared with me that at a women's conference she had received a word of prophecy that she had not shared with me. Like Hannah, she held it in her heart.

True prophecy will come to pass. We are living witnesses. It is not hard for me to believe a word of knowledge or prophecy from someone with an authentic relationship with God. Unlike with our firstborn, I had the honor of naming our daughter. Her name means "example of wisdom." I wanted to make sure that I spoke to her future. I believe it is just as important what we name our children as it is what we call them.

The apostle Paul in his letter to the church at Corinth admonished them to pay attention—to pay attention to the details, to take heed to what they had been taught, to hold on to the truth. He spent a great deal of time with them making sure that they understood the tenets of their faith. With all the negative influences that surrounded them, it was important they had something in them that would sustain them. As scripture states, *"Train up a child in the way he should go: and when he is old, he will not depart from it"* (Prov. 22:6).

Paul took time to teach them. Why? They were going to be responsible for the next generation coming after them. Paul made a clear distinction between instructors and fathers. A father can be an instructor, but not every instructor is a father. What's the difference? The difference is one who teaches by theory/concept and one who teaches by example. Practical teaching is hands-on. Paul demonstrated how the instructors outnumber fathers ten thousand to one. You will always find more folks who will want to tell you what to do than those who can show you what to do.

If I had a dollar for every time I was told, "You are not pastor at home, you are husband and father," I would have a nice little nest egg. I almost bought into that erroneous thinking. I feel sorry for those who have. The truth of the matter is, I am husband and father first, but always the priest of my home. Learning to balance has been the biggest challenge. I cannot just be their pastor at church and never at home. Perhaps that is the reason so many PKs (preachers' kids) have such a disdain for the church, a disdain resultant of the church taking so much from their parents that nothing was left for their family at home. Or maybe it was a parent who did not know when or how to flip the switch. Honestly, it is not hard for me to imagine that anyone who subscribes to the mindset of not being a pastor at home is probably not a pastor anywhere.

The role of fathers in the gospel, though it has suffered significant loss in our times, must never be diminished. It is the father who speaks into his sons and daughters their purpose and identity. One thing I have desired of the Lord is to fulfill my purpose for being. It is my sincere goal to die on empty. I do not want to be buried full of potential and dreams deferred. I do not want to depart from this life without having left an inheritance for my children and a legacy with perpetuity. With the help of the Lord, I have promised not to be a better father to those of the congregation I serve than to those living in my own home. I understand there are certain investments that need to be made in order to see realized the type of returns I want, and any attempt at compensating for time lost or misappropriated is futile.

When those who know the way don't speak up, it puts the ones who don't know the way in a precarious position and at a great disadvantage.

Redeeming the time—

However unintentional our neglect of one child for the other was, it happened. I heard someone say some years ago, "Accidental death is just as dead as intentional death." What do you do when you realize that time spent cannot be recovered? Time is one of the most precious commodities we have. Once it's gone, it's gone. But all is not lost. There is hope.

Communication is key. In our case, having hard conversations, though initially uncomfortable, became our saving grace. Talking about "it" forces the covers to be pulled back. Silence or the absence/lack of communication leaves too much room for false conclusions to be drawn. Thank God that I was able to notice my daughter's behavior changes early on. She began to act out and do things to get our attention. She had my mother there as her primary caregiver in our stead, but it was not the same as having Mommy and Daddy.

Counseling and therapy were seriously frowned upon where I came from. The answer to everything was "pray about it." That sounds good. And don't get me wrong, prayer works when it works. Sometimes additional actions must accompany our prayers. The Bible tells us that faith needs support. *"Even so faith, if it hath not works, is dead, being alone"* (James 2:17). I am a firm believer in utilizing the tools and resources made available to us. I believe it's God's way of providing for us. Accessing resources does not diminish trusting in the source. God works in mysterious ways.

What could have been a wedge that caused irreparable damage was quickly resolved. For that I am eternally grateful. Being home together now is wonderful. Enduring a few months of craziness has been well worth the continued years of bonding and solace. Being far away from our close-knit family, even for a short time, has become hard to do. Being a pastor-dad is an experience, but having a pastor-dad, from what my children tell me, is more of an experience. I've simply reminded them that both of their parents are PKs, so we may know a little something about the experience. We were not allowed to say no too much either.

Passing the test of the pulpit is so much more than being articulate, charismatic, or performance ready. It is not even a matter of being the most studious or most knowledgeable as much as it is being prepared. Being prepared encompasses so much. Being prepared for ministry and life is an ongoing process. As long as you live, there will be more to learn. The more you learn, the more responsible you are to share what you have learned. The more you share what you have learned, the better off the world is and the better you are. Fulfill your purpose. Press forward! Refuse to be silent. You too have a story to tell.

You don't have to get it all, be it all, or do it all. Do your part. Be yourself. Let God be glorified.

Brethren, I count not myself to have apprehended: but this one thing I do, forgetting those things which are behind, and reaching forth unto those things which are before, I press toward the mark for the prize of the high calling of God in Christ Jesus.
(Philippians 3:13–14)

About the Author

Demetrius K. Samu-el, Sr. is a native of Buffalo, New York, who moved to Charlotte, North Carolina, with his new bride, Catherine, nearly twenty-five years ago. In Charlotte he faithfully served as executive assistant to Bishop C. E. Anderson, Sr. at the Sherman Memorial Church of God in Christ for fifteen years. Then he answered the call to start his own ministry, the Shiloh COGIC, a progressive ministry that targeted young professionals, especially those in banking and healthcare.

Pastor Samu-el returned to Sherman Memorial and dutifully served as executive pastor to Bishop C. E. Anderson, Jr. for two years. Upon Bishop Anderson's resignation, Sherman Memorial was without a permanent pastor for nearly six months. Bishop Stenneth E. Powell, Sr., the jurisdictional prelate, served as interim pastor during this transition period.

In March 2015, with the support of the leadership and members of Sherman Memorial, Bishop Powell appointed Elder Samu-el as interim pastor. The bishop returned in June 2015 to formally install Interim Pastor Samu-el as Senior Pastor Samu-el.

Through Pastor Samu-el's leadership, Sherman Memorial's membership has grown, the church had created new ministries, and major capital improvements have been completed with others in progress. The pastor is a student of etymology and numerology, as evidenced by the frequent inclusion of a "word" or "number" lesson during his sermons and Bible study teachings. He has always had a voracious appetite for the Word of God and has dedicated himself to being a lifelong learner humbly seeking to be able to rightly divide the Word of God.

Senior Pastor Samu-el is an astute gospel preacher, a caring pastor, a man of integrity, and a devoted family man. He is a friend to many, a father to a couple, and a husband to one. Faithfulness and stability are hallmarks of this man's character and conduct. Pastor Samu-el is a man who seeks after God. He is a trusted friend and, as all good shepherds do, he is willing to give his all for the flock.

Pastor Samu-el studied journalism/mass communications at St. Bonaventure University and is a career professional with experience in investment banking and healthcare. He is a lifelong learner, currently pursuing advanced degrees in theology and systems management.

Today Senior Pastor Samu-el serves as the fourth pastor and first non-bishop to lead the historic fifty-year-old-plus Sherman Memorial Church of God in Christ in Charlotte, North Carolina.

Pastor Samu-el has lived the ebbs and flows of leading an established congregation through transition, he accepted the challenge of founding a new ministry with a new mission and he has done this in the midst of the most major societal disruptions of this century.

For more information, visit www.dksministries.com.

Printed in the USA
CPSIA information can be obtained
at www.ICGtesting.com
LVHW081643021123
762796LV00003B/61

9 781662 888144